Lookin' at Lava

Poems inspired
by rafting the Grand Canyon of the Colorado

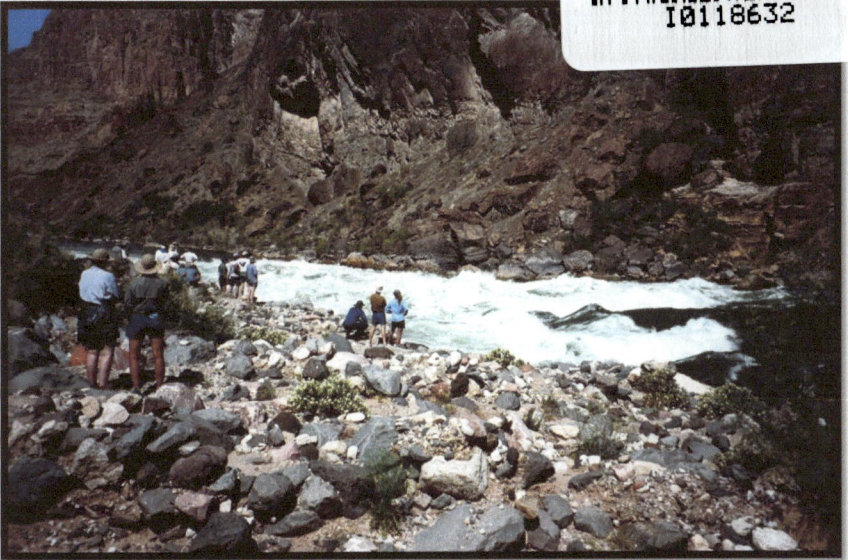

I0118632

by Jenifer Morrissey

For Duffy:
Between Art and STEM
(science, technology, engineering, and math)
there exists but a fine line

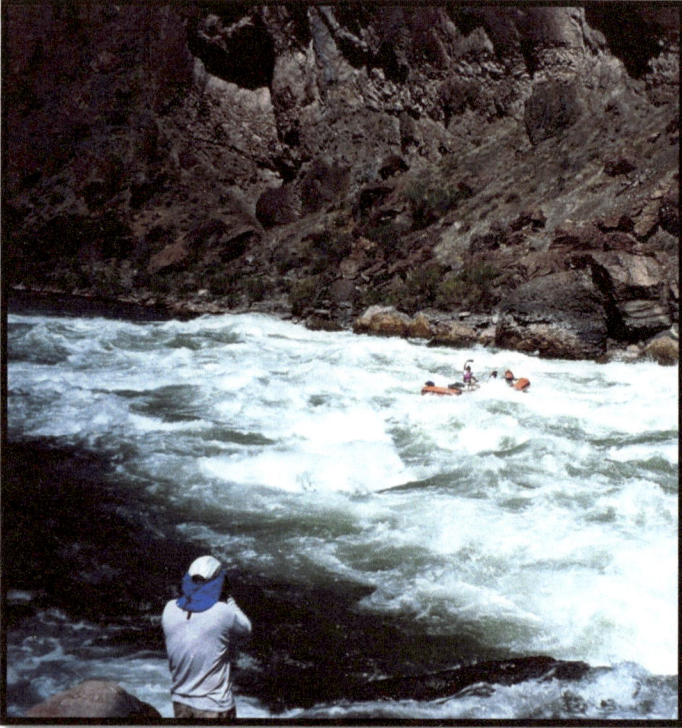

With thanks to Tom Morrissey
from whom I learned to have a photographic eye
making it possible that both our works
could illustrate this book.
And thanks to April Whicker for
her consultation on repairing damaged photos.

ISBN-13: 978-0692442715 (Willowtrail Farm)
ISBN-10: 0692442715

Published in conjunction with createspace.com and
available worldwide on amazon.com

Contents

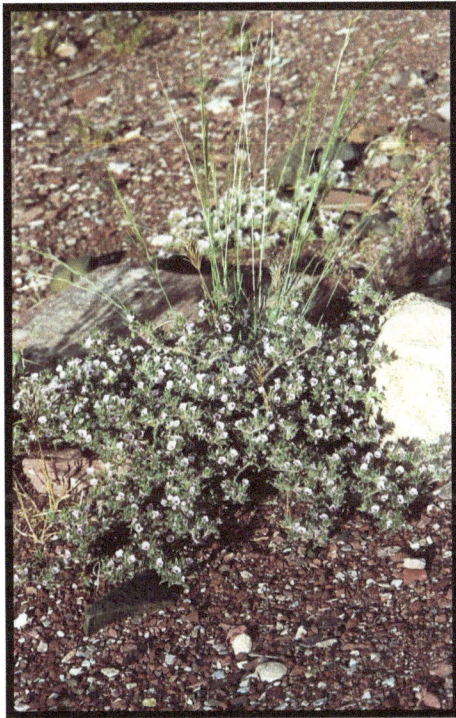

An Adventure Was In Store

It was nineteen-ninety-seven,
And an adventure was in store:
A two week chance to see a canyon
That I'd never seen from its floor.

I'd visited the rim of Grand Canyon
Twice before and been in awe.
But I was soon to learn that the bottom
Abided by a different law.

Celebrating a friend's major milestone
Was the why for this remarkable trip.
A group of friends and our own itinerary
Made for unforgettable fellowship.

It was to be a fourteen day trip;
Many others do it faster.
For that pace I'm ever thankful
For the canyon's layers I could almost master.

Physically it was challenging.
Anxiety made it tough, too.
In the end though the gifts were innumerable,
Leaving me sorry when it was through.

It wasn't the thrill of whitewater
Or the bedazzling beauty around each bend.
It wasn't the 'getting away from it all'
Or reacquainting with more than one old friend.

In the end the river touched me
In ways so deep and profound
That I had to capture the feelings
Before returning to familiar ground.

These poems began pouring from me
As the adventure drew to a close.
They seemed better able to capture
The experience than just simple prose.

Even now so many years later
They take me right back to that place
Both physically on the river
But more importantly a peaceful space

Where it's clear what really matters,
What's important and what's not.
Again I'm extremely grateful
For what the canyon and its river taught.

Descending

(the Colorado River Through Grand Canyon)

A theme of this canyon for me
Has been the act and the art of descending.

The many forms have struck me:

Going down, cutting through.

Flowing, falling, dropping.

The river's descent is a constant,

Flowing mile after mile

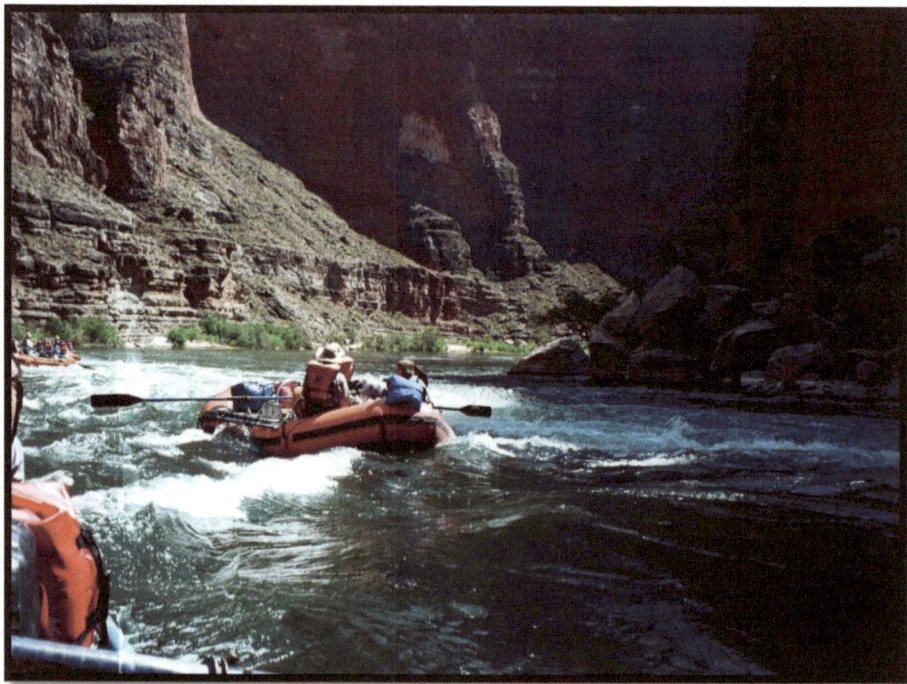

Obviously down and seaward.

Side streams flow, fall, or cascade
Into the surging mainstem.

Rocks have rolled down side canyons to create the roiling rapids.

Whirlpools pull down beneath the river's surface.

Sand finds its way into every nook and cranny.

The trill of a canyon wren's song;

iStock.com/banjoboy02 image #2735866

The act and the art of descending.

The sun's entrance into the canyon each morning.

The dip of a boatman's oar into the river's current.

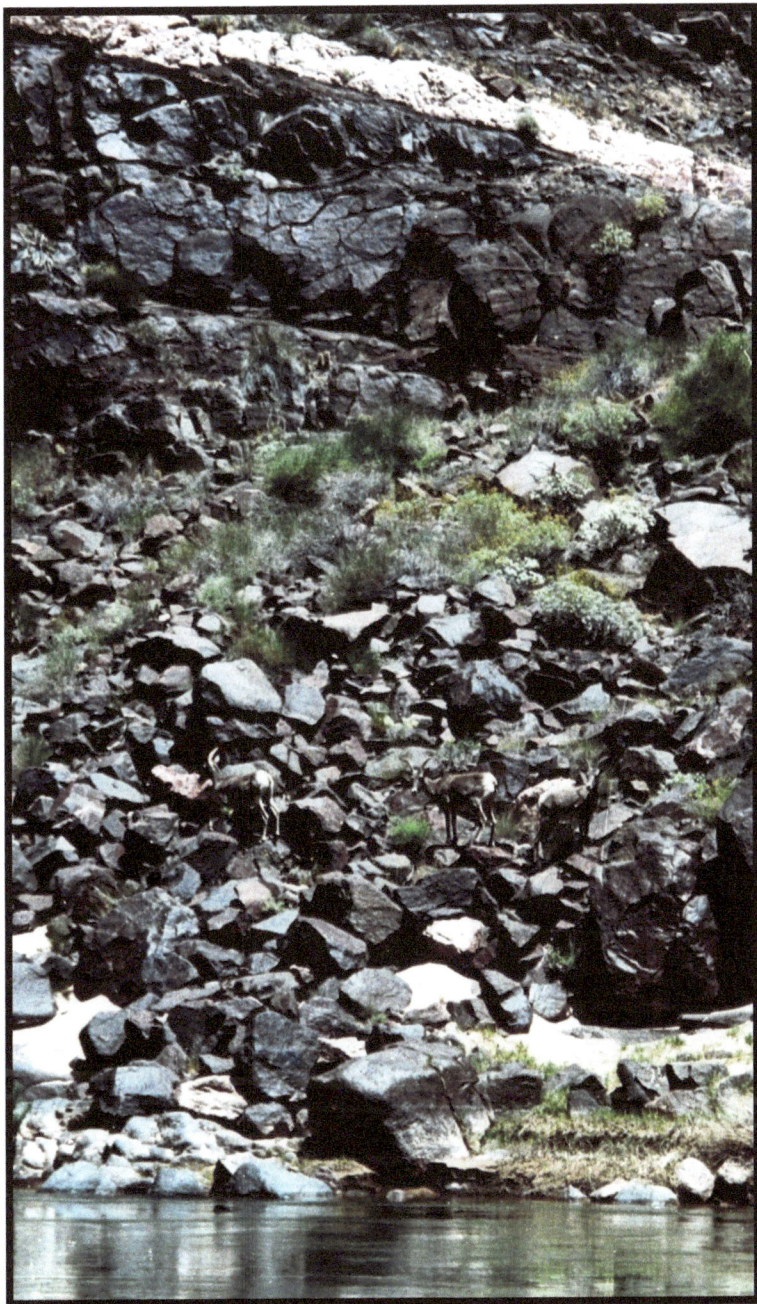

Bighorn sheep and mule deer drawn down to the water's edge.

The deepened voice of approaching white water.

Darkness bringing the day to an end.

Transecting eons of history as told in the layers of rock.

Rare rain drops and the drips of seeps and springs.

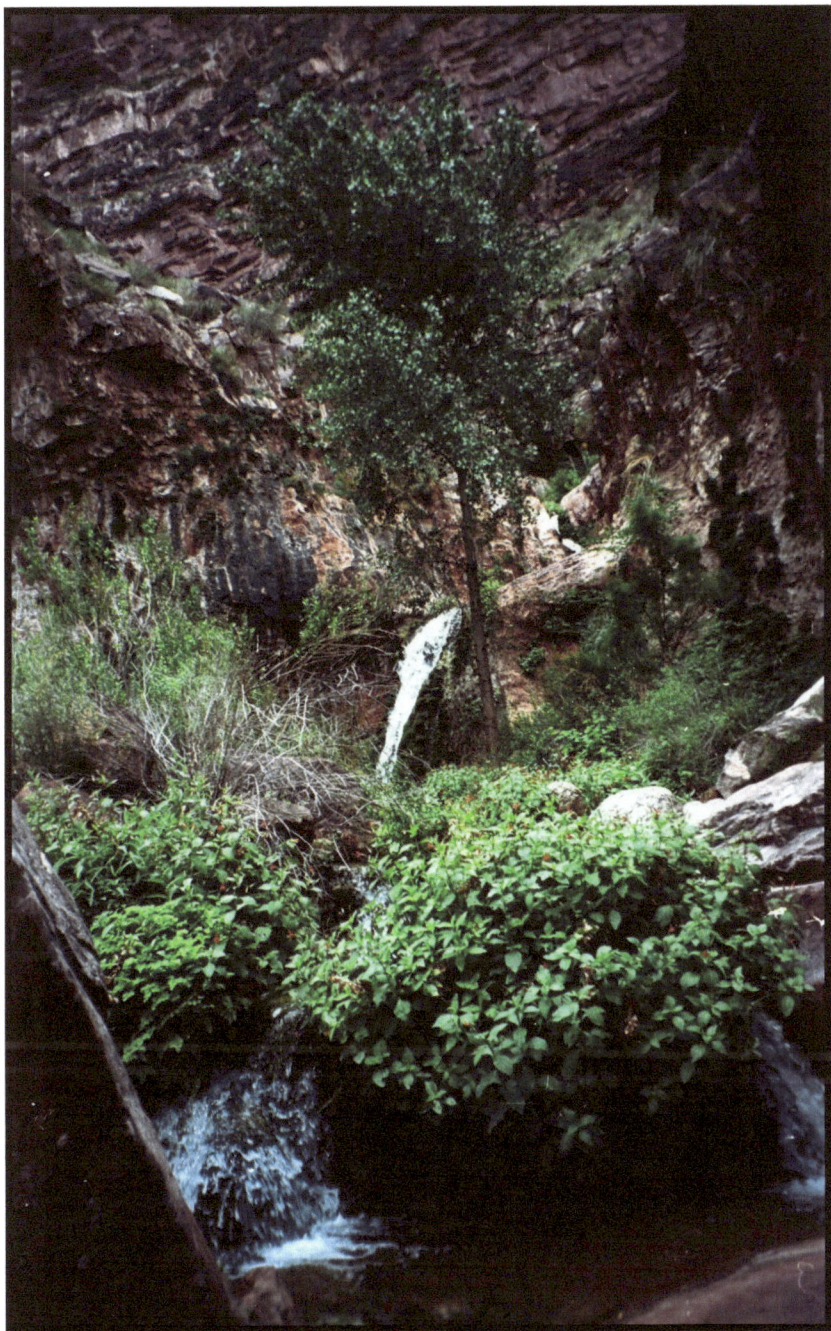

The challenge of the return after an earnest outbound hike.

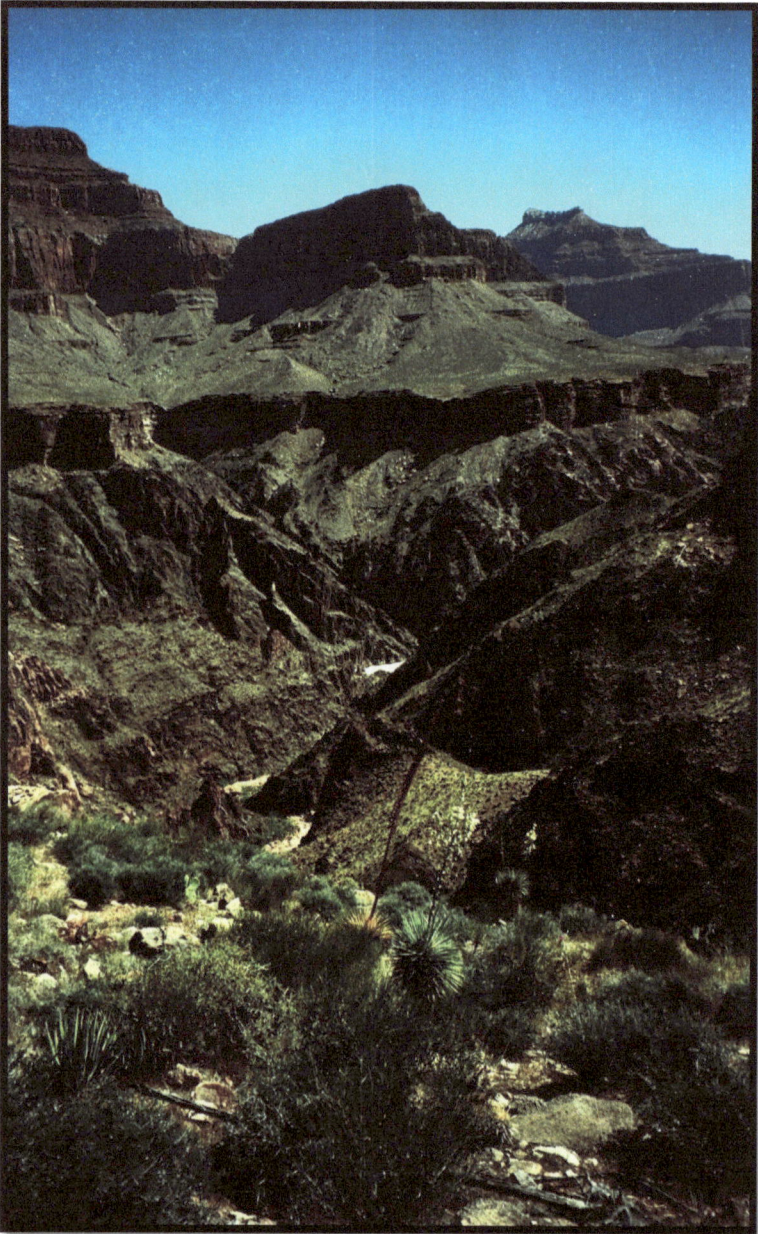

Sinking into a trough before a growing rapid wave.

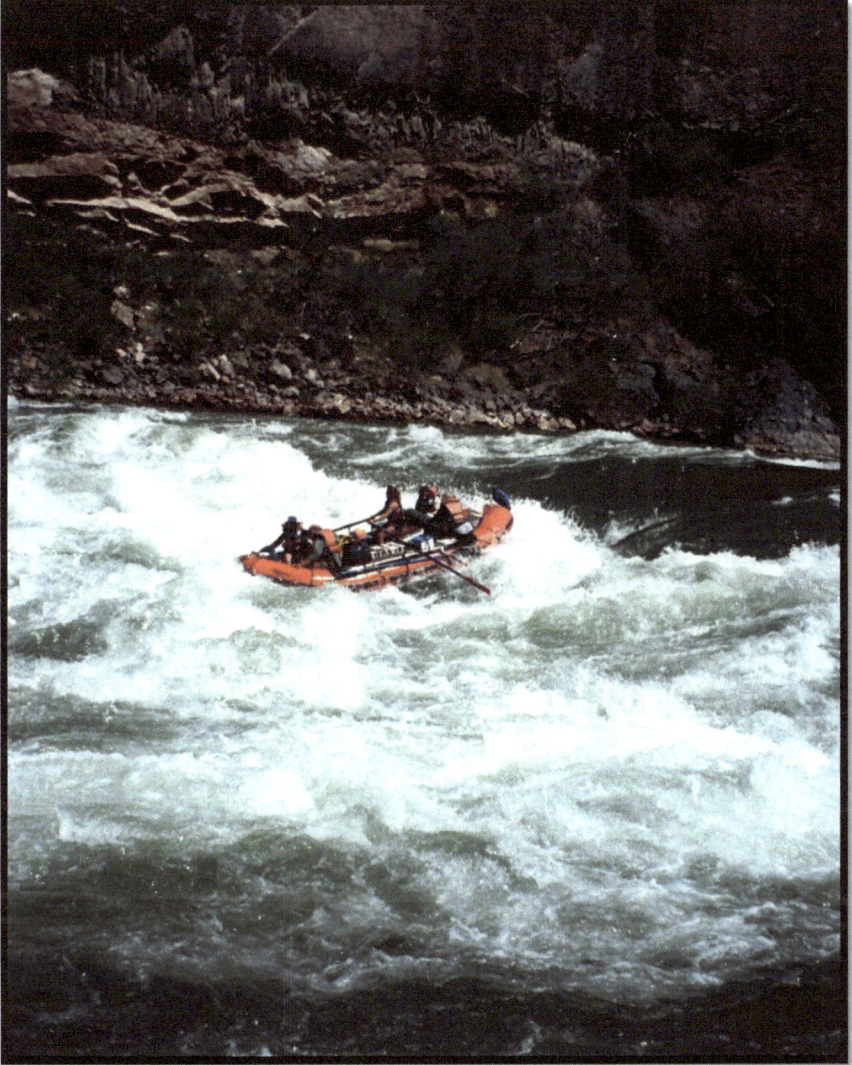

The coloring of the Redwall by red Supai above.

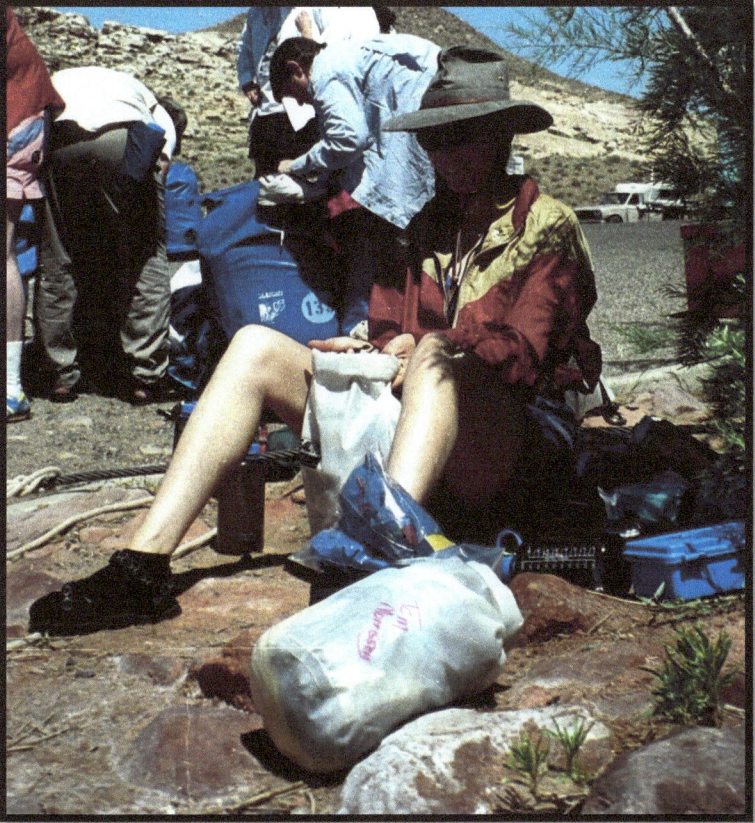

My hat brim set low to the sun's strong glare.

The force of cold water penetrating my hood's imperfect seal.

My body succumbing to the slope of my ill-placed mattress.

Seeking the respite of cooler air down along the water's edge.

Enjoying the act and the art of descending.

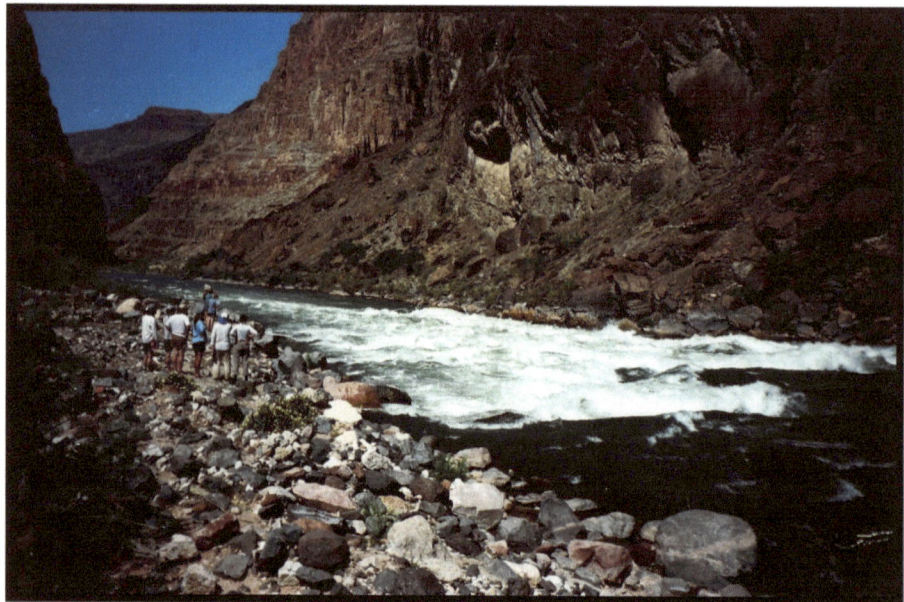

Lookin' at Lava

At the mouth of Prospect Canyon
sits the Lava Rapid Fall.
It's reputation preceded it;
over our group it cast its pall.

Not even explanations
of debris flows historic and new
Could distract us from thoughts of water
and whether we'd make it through.

The nervous energy was palpable
as we stood along the shore,
Listening as the guides shared with us
their Lava Rapid lore.

When finished, they all clustered
with eyes fixed upon the roar,
As we guessed they must be discussing
the ride that was in store.

For me the tension mounted
the longer we stood around.
I had already been convinced
of Lava's ability to astound.

Suddenly two guides peeled off from the rest
and headed back for their boats.
Followed soon by their passengers
donning life vests and some rain coats.

Those left on shore waited patiently
for the pioneers to appear
Upon the river in their rafts
with the rapid looming near.

And there they were, waving energetically,
as the rapid grew in size.
The boats afloat gave us perspective
as they began to dip and rise.

From the view of my inexperienced eye
Lava Rapid then took on new meaning.
For those first boats cruised through the whitewater
with moderate splash and sideways careening.

There were whoops and hollers and hats taken off
to celebrate the joyful ride.
Those on the boats led the rest of us
in letting loose a collective sigh.

Of course for those of us still land-bound
the let-up lasted just an instant.
We realized our time was yet to come
as those first boats became more distant.

Two more guides and their passengers
peeled off for their respective boats.
Our smaller group clustered a little more
and mentally took some notes.

Again my tension mounted
until the boats came into view.
And again Lava loomed large and wild:
an ominous boiling stew.

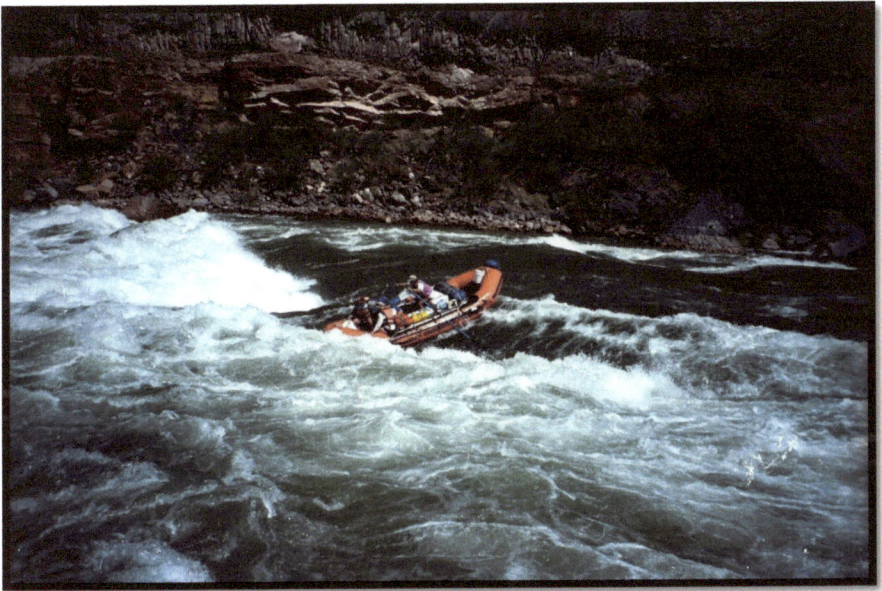

It didn't take long to once again see
orange boats pop out the other side.
More waving hands and shouts of fun
evidence of a successful ride.

My nervousness continued
despite the four successful trips.
I turned away to return upshore
remembering well the swirls and dips.

It was only when we finally launched
that my stomach settled down
And a smile spread across my face,
replacing the nervous frown.

I'm happy to say we did the same
as those boats that went before.
I whooped and hollered and enjoyed myself
much more than when I was ashore.

Postscript

For our boatman Dave there was a special test
in Lava's complex waves.
After a dunking in Hermit farther upstream
he wasn't interested in any close shaves.

He should have known success was imminent, though,
when a gift appeared on the morning run.
After we were downstream, he expressed his delight
and downed the eddy beer in the warm desert sun!

An Artful Geologic Dance

I.

As we have traveled the river
through the canyon in our time,
I have been held captive
by ancient stones of sand and lime
And shale and schist and granite
and everything in between.
My attention has been held by rocks
whose stories I've tried to glean.
Of course I've been held captive
only in the sense that I've been entranced
As I've watched the rocks in the canyon walls
do their artful geologic dance.
Yet "rocks" hardly seems the word to describe
the enduring presence I've been surrounded by.
These canyon walls demand reverence
for the eons they've seen go by.

Geology has always been elusive for me,
what with big words and eras and faults.
Here, though, I've been able to relate to the rocks
with their unconformities, cross-bedding, and vaults.

I think the orderly layers helped
that dominated the first several days.
I learned the character and color of most layers
before they rose into the higher-altitude haze.

Yet learning their form and their substance
isn't really what has captivated me.
It's more how they've felt in relation
and what reflected light has allowed me to see.

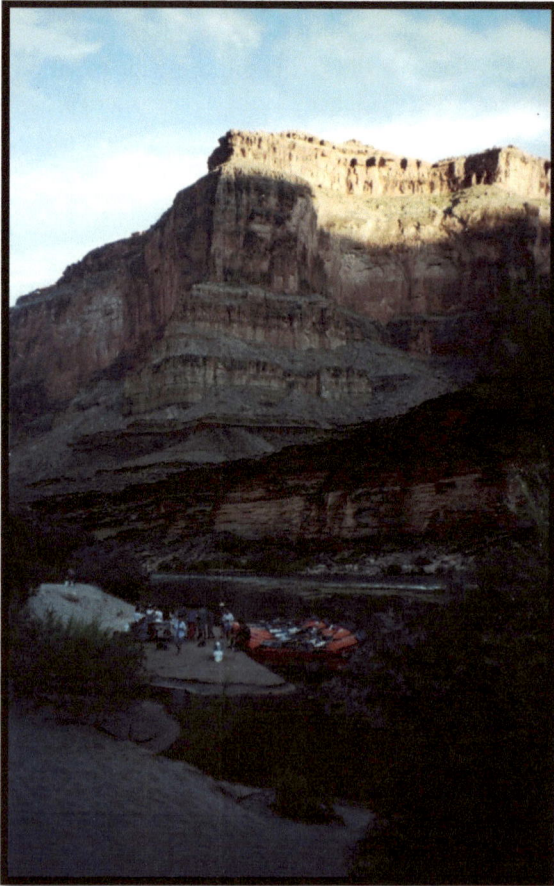

II.
The Kaibab, Coconino, and Hermit
all came quite early in the trip.
But in those first six miles I was most occupied
with getting used to our small rubber "ship."

With those stones and shales and Toroweap, too,
I really didn't have a chance to connect,
Unlike the Redwall that appeared farther downstream
that always appeared to stand so erect.

Those first early layers form the rim of the canyon
or at least that's what we were told,
For the rim was so rarely visible from the river
that their presence was often hard to behold.

The Supai as well seemed distant for me
except for the appellation it inspired for its neighbor.
The red color of its four formations
has been washed down by weather's labor.

The Redwall's sheerness made it striking for me
as did its commanding height.
I could imagine seeking a trail to the rim
and it blocking me, try as I might.

At mile 23, the Redwall emerged;
its earliness creating a constant friend.
I've found I have often gazed up just to see
if it's still there around each canyon bend.

The Muav has been much less striking.
Its blocky look took me days to detect.
And even then it's often surprised me,
but I've still had opportunities to connect.

The Muav is a sedimentary limestone rock
formed from marine life beneath a shallow sea.
The characteristic that's captivated me most, though,
is for the erosion of limestone quite key.

Water easily erodes limestone,
making beautiful pits and concaves.
And the flutes created, some large and some small,
have earned from me many unspoken raves.

I raved with splendor until I was forced
to use the stone as a climbing handhold
For then I found that some water-made art
had sharp edges that caused me to scold!

Mostly, though, I've liked the sculpted appearance
created by limestone and water,
Except when climbing up the creek at Matkat
when lack of footing caused me to totter!

Ah, the Bright Angel! The brightly colored shale
that I enjoyed seeing most when it "cliffed."
The purple, bronze, and green stratifications
were always able to give me a lift.

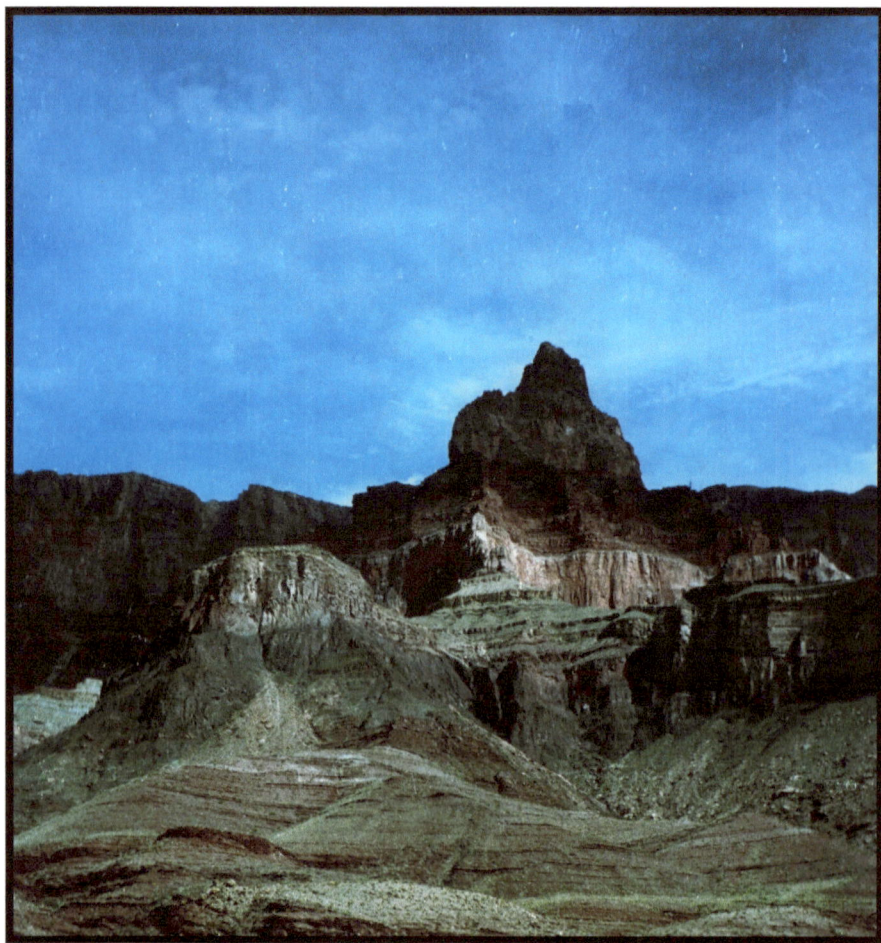

I remember the Tapeats as a typical sandstone,
being gritty and smooth at the same time.
It dominates my memories of Deer Creek and Thunder River
for the challenge it gave to our climb.

Its ledges made for easier upward scrambling
than the preceding cliff-forming limestones.
But the grittiness reminiscent of some coastal beach
made good footing an occasional unknown.

I grew up around sandstone and grit underfoot,
so that didn't bother me much
Except on certain parts of side canyon trails
where we encountered exposure and such.

Then I really worked to continue the hike
keeping my eyes fixed on the trail straight ahead,
And definitely not following the rock I kicked loose
as it sailed down to the distant streambed!

I remember the Tapeats in one other place,
called informally "surface of the moon."
The river sculpted the stone uniquely and smooth.
In my opinion we left there too soon!

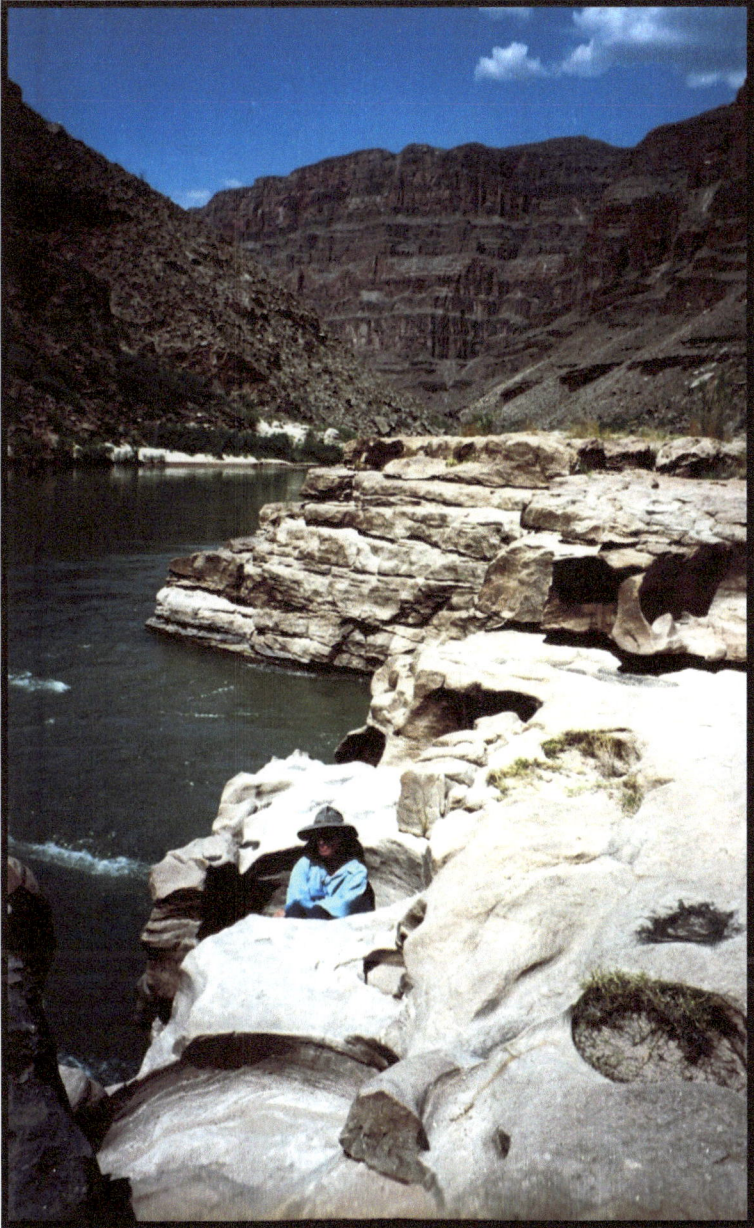

III.

And then there have been the unpredictable rocks
that have easily shattered my geologic grasp.
Bass limestone certainly fits into this group
as does the black rock that made Powell's men gasp.

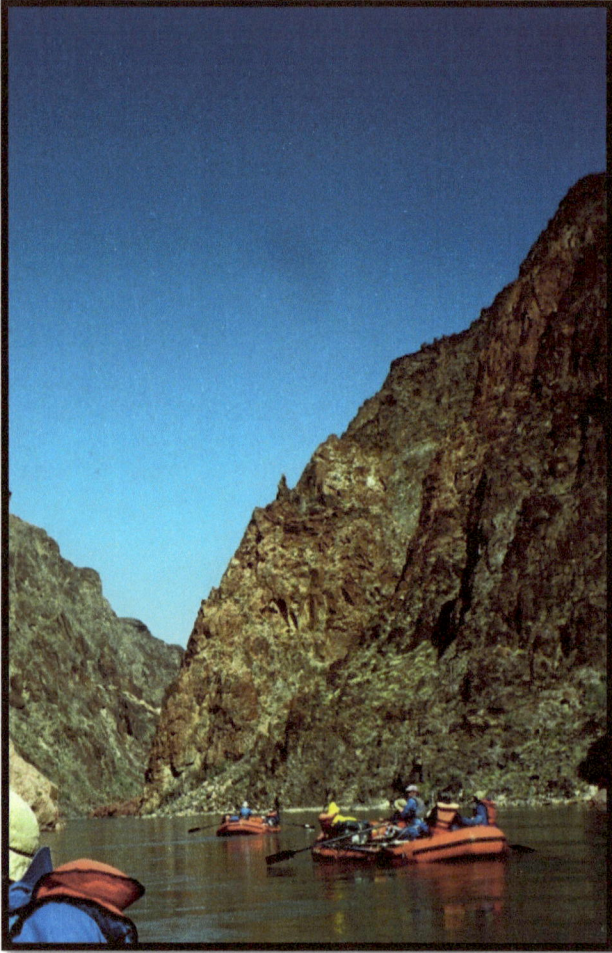

The Bass limestone is amongst the canyon's oldest.
A gray crumbling face ratifies that trait.
Though it has seemed to appear somewhat randomly,
it's ancient erosion that's determined its fate.

After adjusting to narrow canyon walls,
the Dox formation's appearance was profound.
For the canyon opened wide to let the river go through.
By the crumbling rock its flow couldn't be bound.

I liked the maroon rock of the Dox sandstone,
and I liked its loose cinder-like look.
But I admit to being glad it was transient,
for the wide canyon meant heat that could cook!

When we first met the schist and the granite
I learned why those first boatmen felt fear.
For the river narrows down and grows deeper,
and when rapids roar, the danger is near.

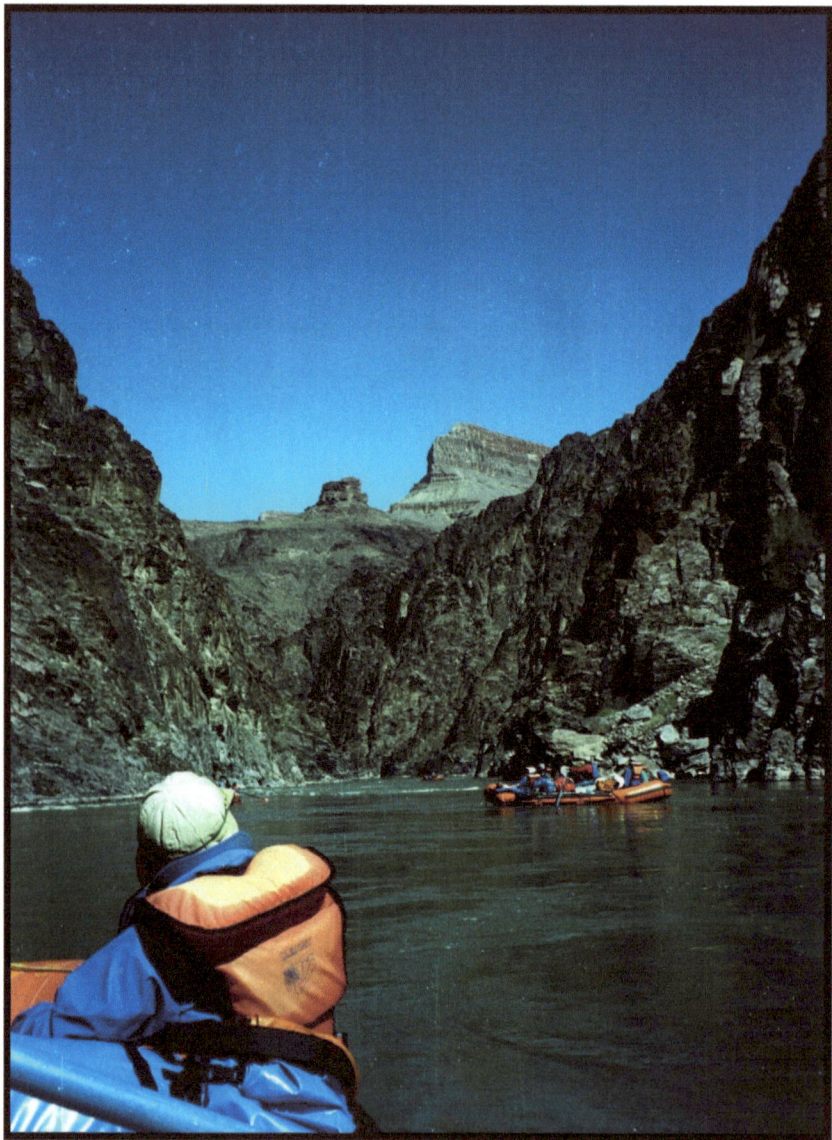

Upper Granite Gorge was the location
where we first encountered these oldest canyon rocks.
Here the river flowed on much too quickly,
for my gaze on the walls tried to lock.

The schist at times was jet black and shiny
and at others "just" gray; dull and light.
The crystalline granite was schist's comrade;
pink and red colors by contrast so bright.

The granite attracted my attention
for the way it snaked up and between.

It intruded upon its schist neighbor
as if wanting always to be clearly seen.

The schist and the granite were like dance partners,
shifting and changing positions in time
To music so slow and so ancient
and creating visual spectacles sublime.

Dispersed through the canyon in proximity to springs
was the flowing, jumbled-looking travertine.
I had a hard time believing it was truly hard rock
for it looked disorderly, like dried mud and lacked sheen.

Also dispersed, yet no doubt for different reasons
was the rusty-cap rock called dolomite.
I knew it in relation to the Bright Angel Shale
and often confused them while enjoying the sight.

One day at the end of a long hike,
I found myself stumbling along
And tiredly griping about boulders
that made my path seem unbearably long.
But when I finally realized
that they were with me, like it or not,
I started appreciating their color
and the day then didn't seem quite so hot.
The boulders were strewn across white sand
which reflected the glorious hues
Of these pieces of each canyon formation
from maroon to indigo blue.
There were reds and grays and violets,
tinged with rust or brown or black.
It seemed to me that a subtle rainbow
was reflected in this long rocky stack.
The beach seemed to be a collection
of all the rocks that had graced us before,
And I marveled again at their beauty
and what I now knew of their lore.

IV.
There came a time when I tired
of guessing right about rocks and then wrong.
Fortunately I was alerted to certain changes
that made my interest become again strong.
I noticed the canyon was changing
the farther west we traveled afloat.
I gave up my attempts at rock labels
and just enjoyed the view from the boat.

The lava rocks were the first indication
that there was still more to be seen.
They appeared continuously along the river for awhile
then later with gaps in between.
The lava rocks were dull on most faces
though the desert sun caused shine on a few.
They appeared as columnar forms stacked together,
as well as blocky chunks piled askew.
It's likely the lava flows dammed the river
and caused it to reconsider its course,
Or to store its erosive power
until it could break through with great force.
In one place we could see up above us
where the river had once had its bed;
Perhaps here the river found a dam daunting
and chose a re-routing instead.
I'm thankful to the relatively young lava,
with its colors of black, brown, and tan
For recapturing my eyes and also my heart
and grounding me in a geologic time span.

V

Here in the lower canyon,
the walls seem tired and old.
They've lost their height and their closeness
and their steepness seems less bold.
The slopes are covered with talus
with an occasional cliff-like rise,
And green dots the flatter sections
bespeaking a seasonal reprise.
Here, the Redwall is altered;
its character has definitely changed.
It's shorter and more crumpled.
My old friend looks new and strange.

The Temple Butte formation dominates
the western canyon's hot, dry walls.
Here the weather is very desert-like,
with few rapids since Lava Falls.
So my thoughts are on the monuments
that this new-to-me limestone forms.
With imagination I can see buttes and temples
whose tops could attract thunderstorms.
The many soft, terraced layers
that here command my attention
Remind me of the roof lines
of Asian buildings used for reflection.
And reflection is motivated in me
once again by a canyon wall,
As I wonder how I could have ever
let my wonder in this place stall.

I'm told the canyon keeps changing
all the way down to Lake Mead.
And I can only imagine the rocks that I'd see
if the river from power dams were freed.

VI

As this trip nears its completion,
I'm convinced of this canyon's place
Amongst the world's great marvels,
for here there's such beauty and grace.
I've felt great awe and wonder
for both the river and the rocks
As I've floated on the water,
and as I've taken quiet walks.
The river flows ever onward
fed by some seemingly inexhaustible source,
And the rocks espouse ancient wisdom
about life and death and time's course.

We've traveled the river slowly,
sensing its rhythm as we've gone;
How it surges and ebbs and changes
and moves the rafts we sit upon.
And I realize it also dances
with the rocks of the canyon walls,
In time always the dominant partner
eroding rock with waterfalls -
Some large and loud and awesome,
some no bigger than a drip -
But still changing the rock of the canyon
with every swirl and dip.

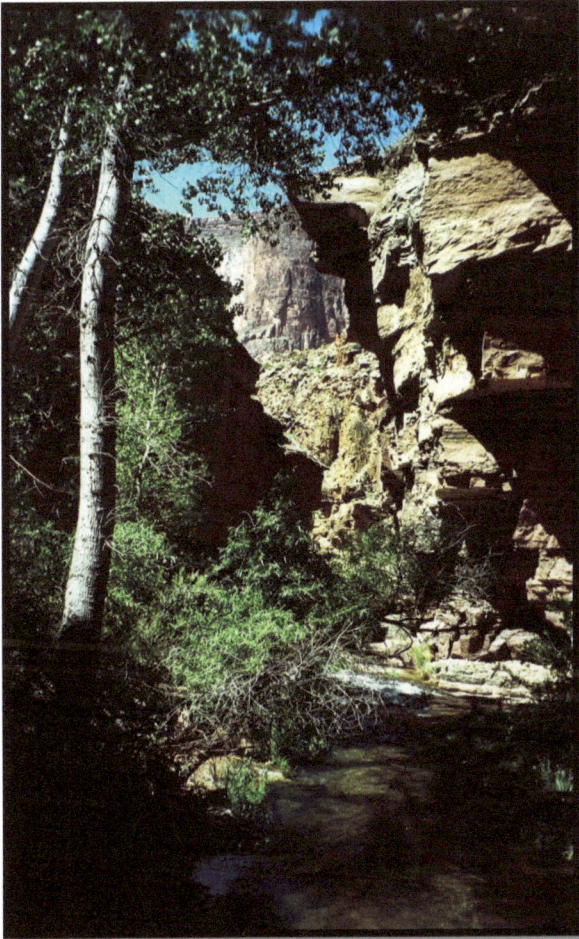

We have followed the river's course
through eons, periods, and eras
As it has moved through schist and granite
as well as sedimentary layers.
Now as we leave the river
I'll take this last precious chance
For one more look at the spectacle
of this artful geologic dance.

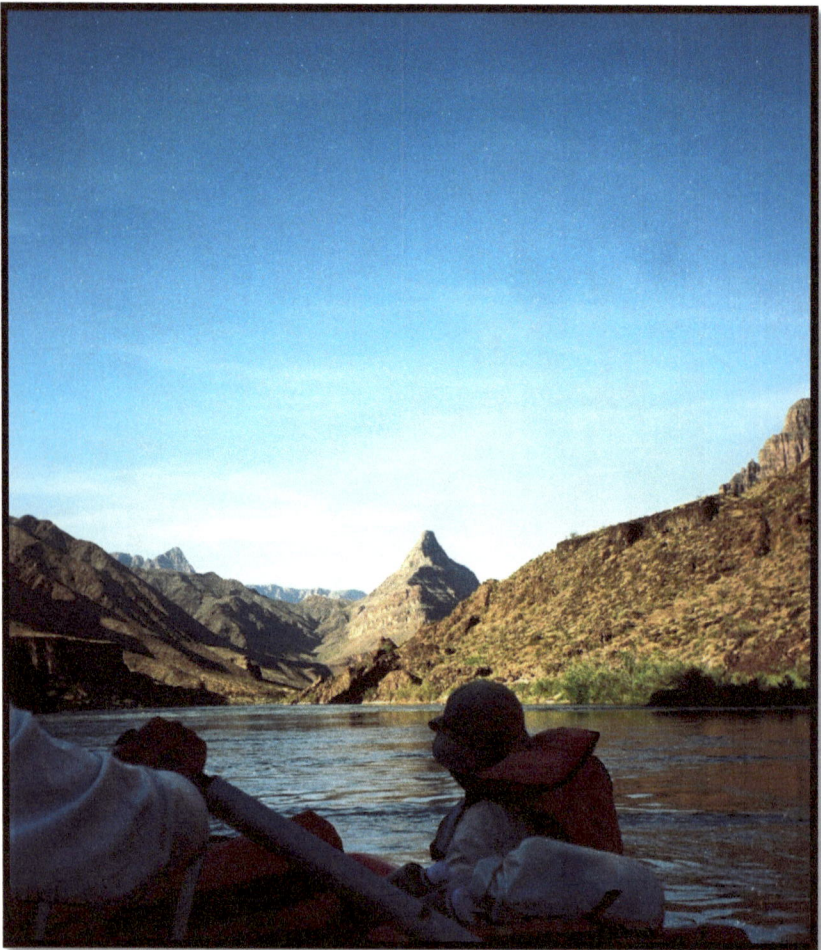

Debarking at Diamond Creek

As I leave the river at Diamond Creek
tears have come to my eyes,
For the river goes on without me
as the last splash on my leg dries.
Suddenly I'm just not ready
for this rafting trip to end.
I want to know what rock is exposed
around that next canyon bend.
I want to hear a rapid's roar
and get wet in the heat of the day.
I want to wonder where we'll be
for our next dinner and overnight stay.

I want to seek cool comfort
from a bath at the river's edge,
And I want to watch a lizard
and see cactus perched upon a ledge.

But there's more to these strong emotions
than wanting more experience for my senses.
There's something else I'm leaving behind
as I return to the world of lawns and fences.
Perhaps I'm yearning for that pace of life
that somehow I could comprehend.
Or the joy of a simplicity of living
that camping can so easily lend.

Perhaps I fear the impending loss
of proximity to the river's free form
Or the awe I've felt at its persistent flow,
though it's just a river's norm

Mostly I suspect, though,
that what I'm leaving behind
Is something even more subtle,
yet something large and infinitely kind.

I think I'm leaving behind
something that has helped me feel somehow whole.
These tears stem from the knowledge that
I'll miss the river singing to my soul

About the Author

Jenifer Morrissey is fascinated by how people interact with the landscapes in which they find themselves. She began writing on the topic for her masters in environmental policy and management from the University of Denver. She owns, with her husband Don Ewy, the logging and construction business Focused on the Forest, LLC.

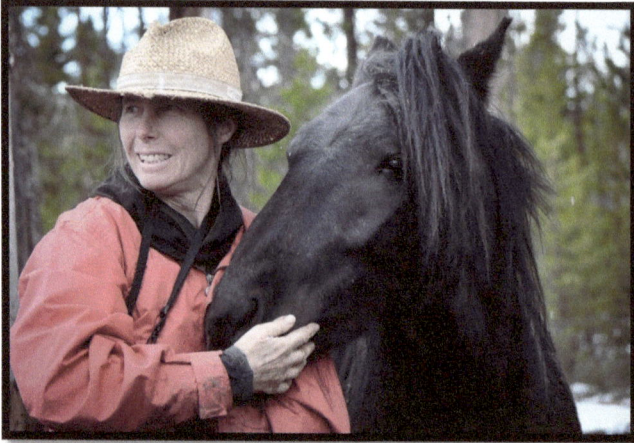

Photo credit Linda Jackson

The author's bachelors in electrical engineering from Stanford University has assisted her in publishing numerous books about the ponies she works and breeds at Willowtrail Farm, ponies which have been shaped by the landscapes of their origin. *Fell Ponies: Observations on the Breed, the Breed Standard, and Breeding* and other titles are available on amazon.com. Her articles have appeared in *Rural Heritage, Driving Digest, Small Farmer's Journal, Heavy Horse World* and other magazines.

www.ingramcontent.com/pod-product-compliance
Lightning Source LLC
Chambersburg PA
CBHW041214270326

41930CB00001B/15